# The Interviews With History Series:

# Jesus , Son Of God

## A Quick Reference Guide

### Doron Alon

# Interviews With History Series: Jesus Son Of God

Alon, Doron.

ISBN: 978-0692593967

**Jesus, Son of God**
–1st ed

Printed in the United States of America
doron@numinositypress.com
Images used for Cover and content:
Cover Created by Shahnaz Mohammed
mailto:NAZNYC@GMAIL.COM
Alexander the Great © v0v - Fotolia.com
Joan Of Arc © Tupungato - Fotolia.com
Ghnegis Kahn © Andrey Burmakin - Fotolia.com
Akhenaten © Travis Hiner - Fotolia.com
Emperor Constantine © Elena Kovaleva - Fotolia.com
Caligula © Aaron Rutten - Fotolia.com
Ancient Jesus Christus Mosaic © philipus - Fotolia.com

http://www.amazon.com/author/doronalon

http://www.interviewswithhistory.com

# DEDICATION
To my late Grandmother Dorothy Meyer. I love you.

# CONTENTS

# INTRODUCTION

When one looks back in ancient history, there are a few luminaries that stand out. Luminaries that shook the world so intensely that their influence has never abated until this day. We have Alexander the Great and the spread of Hellenism. Abraham who laid the foundation for the major Semitic religions. Socrates, Plato and Aristotle who taught us how to use our minds. And so many others.

In this book we will be discussing the life of arguably the most influential person in history; Jesus. Whether you believe Jesus truly existed as a flesh and blood human being or as simply an archetype representing an idea, there is no doubt that Jesus changed the world with his teachings.

In saying that, I would like to point out that this book will not argue for or against the historicity of Jesus, which is for you, the reader to decide. Our goal in the Interviews with History series is to provide concise and easy reference guides to major historical figures using the texts that represent them. With that in mind, we will be discussing Jesus' life in context of the New Testament, more specifically the gospels of Mathew, Mark, Luke and John. I will use the New International Version as my bible of choice. We will be covering key points of his life that I feel represents Jesus' key message. For more detailed view of his teaching I suggest reading the four gospels in their entirety.

I am hoping that through this book and through the Interviews with History Series in general, that you, the reader, will learn something new. That is my intention. Now, let us take a walk through time.

# CHAPTER 1: THE MESSIANIC ETHOS

One of the hardest tasks of historical analysis that we often encounter is the placing of events in time. Certainly the ancients did not view history the way we do now. Before the modern conventions of B.C and A.D, time was recorded in a variety of different ways. In many ways our western way of viewing history is pragmatic in nature and is used as a general tool to place events in history. In terms of accuracy, it is not 100% accurate. The current year as of this writing is 2013. In our conception of history that means 2013 years after Jesus' birth. Even the staunchest secular historians still use the same dates. Instead of referring to B.C as Before Christ, in academic circles it is referred to as "Before the Common Era" to demarcate the same time period.

In either case, 1 A.D is the starting point and just so happens to be the year of Jesus' birth according to some religious historians. It is more likely he was born around 6-4 B.C. In many ways this is an artificial device since we cannot pinpoint his exact birth year with any degree of accuracy. The issue of dating Jesus' birth still rages on to this day. Clearly, Jesus was a major figure in history. Our entire conception of time is couched around him. Whether he was born on December 25, Year 1 is not clear. For the sake of simplicity we will use the accepted dates and the conventional norms in terms of historical chronology; B.C is before Christ and A.D (Anno Domini: year of Our Lord) for after Christ.

In this chapter we will be discussing in brief the times in which Jesus was born. Before I proceed, however, I'd like to go back a little further so as to get a broader view of the times he will later find himself in. History doesn't happen in a vacuum. Jesus was born into a time that was rife with Messianic fervor. In this way, Jesus was born exactly at the right time

Jesus was born in what is now modern day Israel. During the early Iron Age, about 1020-1030 B.C, this land was initially divided into 2 major regions. The southern part was ruled by the Kingdom Of Judah and the northern part by the Kingdom of Israel. Although they shared religious beliefs and for the most part shared ethnic ties, they squabbled from time to time. In 720 B.C the Kingdom of Israel was ransacked by the Neo-Assyrian Empire. The Kingdom of Judah was barely independent; they paid tribute to the Assyrian Empire. As the Assyrian Empire waned, Judah regained much of its true independence. However, this would not last long. Around 610-609 B.C they had to pay tribute once again, but to another great empire; the Ancient Egyptians. This too would not last forever and eventually the Babylonians wrestled Judah from Egyptian hands which led to a brutal occupation in which many Jews were exiled from the land.

Luckily for the Jews at the time, the cruel rule of Babylon would eventually come to an end when Cyrus the Great, leader of the Persian Empire would defeat Babylon around 539 B.C. Cyrus was very good to the Jews; he was mentioned at least 23 times in the Old Testament and all in glowing terms. Some even implied that he was a messiah of sorts. Persian Rule would extend for about 207 years.

Now here is where things start to get interesting. Eventually the Persian Empire would fall to Alexander the Great, who ushered in the Hellenistic Empire and then after Alexander, the Seleucid Empire (167-160 B.C). There were a few major skirmishes in between, but for the sake of this text I will cover the ones I feel are relevant to our discussion.

Around 160-140 B.C The Seleucid Empire was crumbling and full revolt was taking place, led by the Jewish Warrior Judah the Maccabee. This Revolt was known the Maccabean Revolt. Eventually the Maccabees were successful and they started to purge the Jewish temple of Greek Statuary. This revolt ushered in a time of a kind of Jewish revivalism and self rule. Jewish practices that were previously banned under the Seleucid Empire were now reinstated.

Around 63 B.C the Romans eventually brought Israel under their control and it stayed like that for several hundred years. Now Rome often used local leaders as representatives of the people so during the years 37 B.C to 1 B.C they chose Herod the Great to be a kind of puppet king. He was the king during the birth of Jesus; it was under his successor Herod Antipas that Jesus was crucified.

During the Roman occupation before and during Jesus time there were several movements that promised to liberate the Jews from Roman occupation. Most of them were crushed or simply lost steam and never went anywhere. Messianic rumors were constantly in the air. People were desperate for salvation and looked for signs that one day they will be saved from brutal occupation.

It was this environment that Jesus found himself in. He was in the center of it all. Due to the fact that the Jewish people have such a long history under the rule of foreign occupation, a strong Messianic Ethos existed and many people tapped into this. During Jesus' time, it hit its nadir.There were many itinerant preachers during that time claiming to have the answer, but few lived to realize their aspirations. As time went on, countless messiah wannabes came and went. This time, however, things were going to be different. Enter Jesus.

# CHAPTER 2: THE STAR OF BETHLEHEM: THE BIRTH OF JESUS

The first book of the New Testament is the book of Matthew, and for good reason. It is the only gospel that has the Jesus genealogy front and center. Although the gospels of Luke also touches on the genealogy, it isn't until chapter 3. Having the genealogy front and center was very important. The gospel of Mathew was meant to establish the linage of Jesus. Lineage is important throughout the bible. It is even more so when it relates to Jesus.

The Jewish people have always believed that the messiah would come from the blood line of King David. Since the gospels teach that Jesus is the messiah it was important to be able to trace Jesus back to the bloodline. The book of Mathew does this (Chapter 1:1-18). In light of this, we will start our travel through Jesus' life starting with the book of Mathew.

It was around spring, 1 AD or 4 BC, depends who you ask that the young girl Mary and her betrothed Joseph the carpenter were soon to be married. Mary was a virgin and was thus without children. It is not clear whether Joseph had children before his marriage to Mary. Some sources outside of the New Testament, (mainly the Catholic Church) state that perhaps Joseph was a widower and had children from a previous marriage. This was ascertained because in the New Testament, Jesus is said to have had 4 brothers and sisters. The texts do not mention how many sisters he had. They could not have been Mary's since she was a virgin. So it makes sense that they would be Josephs. The jury is still out on that. It is possible these are Mary's kids after Jesus was born.

Joseph and Mary were betrothed but before they could consummate their union a dreadful discovery was made. Mary, the Virgin, was pregnant and it was not Joseph's child. In Jewish tradition a woman who got pregnant out of wedlock was punished very harshly, maybe even killed. Joseph, who was a religious man himself and much older than Mary had a tremendous amount of angst about this. This could ruin him as well. He wanted to quickly and quietly get a divorce. He did not want to expose her or himself for that matter to any kind of attention or drama.

One night, as he lay wracked with worry he manages to get to sleep. He has a dream that would make his decision as to whether to divorce Mary or not. In Mathew 1:20-21 it states "...An Angel of the Lord appeared to him in a dream, and said" Joseph, Son of David, do not be afraid to take Mary home as your wife, because what is conceived in her is from the Holy Spirit. She will give birth to a son, and you are to give him the name Jesus* because he will save his people from their sins" (*Jesus in Hebrew is Joshua which means 'a savior; a deliverer').

After this dream he felt more assured and did what the angel told him. They were not to consummate their union until she was to give birth to Jesus.

**The Birth of Jesus:**

Close to the time of Jesus birth the Roman Emperor Caesar Augustus issued a decree that a census should be taken throughout the entire Roman world. In order for this to take place people needed to go back to their respective hometowns. In order for Joseph to be counted he had to go back to Bethlehem, the town of King David. Since Mary was pledged to Joseph, he brought her with him so she could be counted in the census. This was not the most opportune time, Mary was very pregnant and in those days child birth was fraught with dangers. Traveling over an inhospitable landscape and being pregnant wasn't exactly ideal...But it had to be done.

They arrive in Bethlehem and Mary was in labor. They searched and searched for a guest room or some place where she could give birth, but to no avail. Eventually there was a place, but they only had room in the barn. This would have to do; Jesus was ready to enter the world. She gave birth, wrapped him in a cloth and had to place him in a manger.

**The Star in the East:**

During and after Jesus' birth, a major sign would appear in the sky that would foretell of his arrival; the arrival of a great savior of the Jewish people. A bright star shone in the sky and wise men (also known as the Magi) from the east would interpret this celestial event as a sign that a King was born. It is not 100% clear where these wise men came from, but it is clear they came from the east. Both Persia and Babylon had very extensive astrological systems which leads me to believe that perhaps they came from that region. There were 3 wise men, so perhaps they each came from different places of origin. The New Testament does not make this clear.

As they traveled the vast inhospitable desert, they used this star as a beacon. This Star eventually leads them to Bethlehem where this predicted savior was to be born. The Wise men, not realizing fully that the current King of the Jewish people, Herod, was merely a corrupt aristocrat, they came and asked him where the child was. Herod was certainly not interested in anyone who would redeem the Jewish people. Far from it, when the wise men approached him and told him of the star they had seen and that it indicates a savior was born, Herod was not happy. But he pretended to be very interested and happy that a Savior was born. He tried to convince the Wise men to find the New Born King and tell him where he was so he could go and give praise. In reality however, he wanted the child killed so as not to have any competition.

Herod was no stranger to political intrigue, ruthlessness and the ordering of assassinations. He lived in a time when the Romans killed their own family members in order to maintain power, so it is understandable that Herod wanted any potential rival out of the way, no matter how old they were. Although Herod had Jewish roots, he was decidedly Roman in the way he ruled. This becomes very obvious after Jesus is born.

The Magi go on their way. They eventually find Jesus and offer up three gifts; Gold, Frankincense and Myrrh. These seem like unusual gifts to the modern day person, but in those days those 3 gifts were incredibly valuable. Some would argue that the Frankincense and Myrrh may have been even more valuable than the gold at the time. Incense was a very hot commodity throughout the ancient world. As the Magi were set to leave they receive a dire warning from God that they should not tell Herod where the child is for surely he would kill him. They were also told to take another route back to their countries of origin so not to be spotted by Herods Hentchmen.

Herod eventually comes to the realization that he has been duped, the Magi never return and this causes him to fly off into a rage. He was committed to killing this newborn king. The problem he faced was daunting. It was then he made a horrendous decision. He thought, "Well, if I can't find the new born child who would be king, I will order the massacre of all boys in Bethlehem between the ages of 2 and under". And that is exactly what he does. Before this decree could be carried out, an angel of God came to Joseph in a dream and told him to leave Bethlehem with Mary and Jesus and go to Egypt until further notice.

The gospels may differ in terms of the timing of events so it is not clear how soon after Jesus birth this decree came to be. The fact that Herod issued the slaughter of boys 2 and under indicate that perhaps 2 years may have passed between the Magis meeting with him and the decree to the massacre of the boys of Bethlehem.

**"I brought My Son Out of Egypt"**

As I stated earlier, the exact timing of these events is not clear. The duration of their stay in Egypt is also not clear, but what is clear is that they were to return upon Herod's death. Instead of returning to Bethhelem they eventually settled in Nazareth. Apparently Herod's son was not someone they wanted to encounter on their way back.

Fast forward a few years and it starts becoming clear that Jesus was an exceptional boy, now aged 12. Every year during the Passover festival, people from all over Israel would come to Jerusalem to celebrate. Jesus' parents were no exception. As the festivities were coming to a close, Joseph and Mary prepared to return to Nazareth, they go looking for Jesus but he is nowhere to be found. After three days of relentless searching they find him sitting in the temple courts, sitting among the teachers listening to them and asking questions. Everyone who had a chance to hear him was astounded by his depth and erudition. When his parents arrived they rebuked him slightly asking him why he had just disappeared like that. He answered "Why have you been searching for me? Didn't you know I had to be in the father's house?" Joseph and Mary did not quite understand what he meant, but those words were a hint and perhaps a warning of what was to come in his life.

# CHAPTER 3: YOU ARE MY SON, WHOM I LOVE; WITH YOU I AM WELL PLEASED

Jesus began his ministry when he was about 30 years old. As you can see there is quite a gap in his history. He goes from being a young boy to being a man within just a few verses. The main gospels or Canonical gospels themselves tell very little of this time. However, there are other gospels that were not included in the official canon that claim to fill in those gaps. Those are called the infancy Gospels. In the Interviews with History Series ; a title is in the works that will cover Jesus as he was portrayed in the infancy gospels.

Before Jesus was to start his ministry however he needed to be baptized. In those days a man by the name of John the Baptist (who was Jesus' cousin) was gaining popularity. It appears that Jesus was part of John the Baptist's entourage. John was an itinerant preacher whose scathing words towards the establishment brought much attention to him. It was his outspokenness that eventually lands him in prison and eventually gets him killed.

John was clearly an ascetic and lived in a way that shunned worldly goods. His clothes were made out of camels hair; he wore a leather belt around his waist. His diet consisted of mainly locust and wild honey...Delicious!

John was so revered that people from all over the country came to be baptized by him. He truly had the divine presence in him. Although many had viewed John the Baptist as being the Messiah, John clearly sees that Jesus is the one predicted to be the savior. He states that one will come that will be greater than he and goes on to say " But after me comes one who is more powerful than I, whose sandals I am not worthy to carry..."

As people approached John one at a time to be baptized eventually it was time for Jesus to be baptized. When Jesus presented himself to John; John was hesitant, he looks at Jesus and says "I need to be baptized by you, and you come to me?" Clearly John realized that Jesus was the Messiah that all the prophecies had foretold. Jesus, however, insisted that John go through with the baptism.

It was at his baptism that he officially emerges as a new man. He is, at that moment, anointed by God as the savior. As he emerged from the water, the heavens open up and he saw the spirit of God descending from heaven like a Dove and illuminating him. It was at this point he hears "This is my Son, whom I love; with him I am well pleased."

The Baptism was truly the turning point in Jesus' mission. It is now that he starts his ministry with full force.

# CHAPTER 4: JESUS THE TEACHER AND MIRACLE WORKER

**The Devil Tests Jesus:**

After his anointing, Jesus was called into the wilderness for forty days to pray and meditate in order to further purify his soul for the difficult mission he was about to embark upon. During this time angels attended to him and he lived solely by divine sustenance. It was during his wanderings in the desert when Satan, the great adversary was to test Jesus' resolve.

Satan approaches Jesus with a series of questions that he hopes will cause Jesus to turn his back on God and his mission. Jesus, being in a weakened state due to fasting would be in a vulnerable state and Satan knew this.

Satan says" If you are the Son of God, tell these stones to become bread."

Jesus answered, "It is written: 'Man shall not live on bread alone, but on every word that comes from the mouth of God."

Then Satan took him to the holy city of Jerusalem and had him stand on the very highest point of the temple. He tells Jesus to throw himself off the highest point and see if God will save him.

Jesus cleverly replied "Do not tempt the Lord thy God"

Satan was persistent and was intent on breaking Jesus and appealing to Jesus' human nature. So took him to a very high mountain and showed him all the kingdoms of the world and the abundance that they have. Satan being "Lord of the earth" says to Jesus "All this I will give you," he said, "if you will bow down and worship me."

Jesus finally has enough and says, "Away from me, Satan! For it is written: 'Worship the Lord your God, and serve him only."

Satan eventually gives up, realizing that Jesus will not fall so easily, but it won't be the last time Satan will encounter Jesus. It was only a matter of time.

The testing of Jesus is very important, it shows that Jesus had true faith and resolve and in many ways it is a testament to the fact that he was truly a man of God. Any other person would have easily fallen to the slings and arrows of outrageous fortune that Satan was offering. Jesus passed the test and was now ready to go out into the world and teach and reveal who he really was.

**Jesus Announces the Good News:**

During this time, John the Baptist was imprisoned as mentioned earlier. When Jesus heard that John had been put in prison, he withdrew to Galilee. He really had no choice.He knew that anyone associated with John might be hunted by Herod. Jesus leaving Nazareth went and lived in Capernaum, which was by the lake in the area of Zebulun and Naphtali which is located in northern Israel to fulfill what was said through the prophet Isaiah:

"Land of Zebulun and land of Naphtali,the Way of the Sea, beyond the Jordan, Galilee of the Gentiles-the people living in darkness have seen a great light;on those living in the land of the shadow of death a light has dawned."

Once there, Jesus declares the good news. He declared to the world" The time has come," he said. "The kingdom of God has come near. Repent and believe the good news!" That was it; this was the point of no return.

**Jesus Calls His First Disciples:**

As Jesus walked beside the Sea of Galilee, he saw Simon who who Jesus would name Peter and his brother Andrew casting their nets into a lake, the two were fishermen. He says to them "Come, follow me, and I will send you out to fish for people." Oddly enough, that is all they needed to hear, they abandoned their nets and followed him. He walked a little farther, and he saw James son of Zebedee and his brother John in a boat, preparing their nets, they too were apparently fishermen. He called them to join him, and they left their father Zebedee in the boat with the hired men and followed him.

I would like to point out that the gospels' account of the Jesus quest for disciples are in conflict. In John it states that Andrew overheard John the Baptist call Jesus the Messiah, the Lamb of God and that some of Johns Students followed Jesus. Andrew went to look for his brother Peter and they went and followed Jesus. This account is very different from Matthew and Mark. As with many ancient texts, there is often some discrepancy, in either case, it is clear that Jesus' movement was starting to grow.

The next day, Jesus decides to leave. On his way, he finds Philip, and urged him to"Follow me."Philip, like Andrew and Peter, was from the town of Bethsaida. Philip then found Nathanael and told him, "We have found the one Moses wrote about in the Law, and about whom the prophets also wrote—Jesus of Nazareth, the son of Joseph." Nathanael being somewhat of a skeptic and a cynic I might add did not beileve it. He says "Nazareth! Can anything good come from there?" Apparently Nazareth was not known to be the most exciting town in the world.

Philip convinces Nathanel to come and see for himself. When Jesus saw Nathanael approaching, he said of him, "Here truly is an Israelite in whom there is no deceit." Nathanael asked" How do you know me?"

Jesus answered, "I saw you while you were still under the fig tree before Philip called you."

Then Nathanael amazed said, "Rabbi, you are the Son of God; you are the king of Israel."

Jesus said, "You believe because I told you I saw you under the fig tree. You will see greater things than that." He then added, "Very truly I tell you, you will see 'heaven open, and the angels of God ascending and descending on the Son of Man." This statement is very powerful and probably stunned his growing cadre of followers. They have not seen anything yet.

Eventually Jesus would appoint 12 apostles: Simon (whom he named Peter), his brother Andrew, James, John, Philip, Bartholomew, Matthew, Thomas, James son of Alphaeus, Simon who was called the Zealot, Judas son of James, and Judas Iscariot, who eventually betrays Jesus and becomes one of the most reviled people in history.

**Jesus Rejected at Nazareth**

Jesus returns to Galilee and the news about him spread like wildfire throughout the countryside. He was teaching in their synagogues, a risky move, but people praised him.

He went to Nazareth, where he had been brought up, and on the Sabbath day he went into the synagogue, as was his custom. He stood up to read, from the scroll of the prophet Isaiah; it said "The Spirit of the Lord is on me, because he has anointed me to proclaim good news to the poor. He has sent me to proclaim freedom for the prisoners and recovery of sight for the blind, to set the oppressed free, to proclaim the year of the Lord's favor."

He stops and paused and goes on to say "Today this scripture is fulfilled in your hearing."

The people were dumbfounded and amazed at how eloquently he spoke. Some inquired about him and recognized him and they asked "Isn't this Joseph's son?"

It was at this point that things were about to turn ugly. Jesus said to them, "Surely you will quote this proverb to me: 'Physician, heal yourself!' And you will tell me, 'Do here in your hometown what we have heard that you did in Capernaum. "

"Truly I tell you," he continued, "no prophet is accepted in his hometown. I assure you that there were many widows in Israel in

Elijah's time, when the sky was shut for three and a half years and there was a severe famine throughout the land. Yet Elijah was not sent to any of them, but to a widow in Zarephath in the region of Sidon. And there were many in Israel with leprosy in the time of Elisha the prophet, yet not one of them was cleansed—only Naaman the Syrian."

He essentially said that the people of Nazareth were without faith and they would not see miracles and that only those, even non-Jews with faith would receive miracles, but not them, the chose faithless.

The people in the synagogue were so angered when they heard this. They had murder on their minds. They all got up and wanted to drive him off a cliff. But he walked right through the crowd and went on his way.

Although the people were ready for a savior, it was frowned upon to call oneself the "fulfillment" of scripture. This was considered the height of blasphemy and it was for this reason they wanted to kill him.

## Jesus the Miracle Worker

After Jesus' near fatal encounter with the people in the first synagogue he visited, he remained steadfast and continued to preach in the synagogues. Jesus went throughout Galilee, teaching, proclaiming the good news of the kingdom, and started healing all kinds of diseases that people had. Understandably, the news about him spread all over. People in Syria, brought him their sick as well as those who were demon-possessed. He healed pretty much any kind of illness.  Huge, crowds from Galilee, Jerusalem, Judea and the region across the Jordan gathered around him.

It is here that Jesus' most famous **Sermon on the Mount** took place.

The Sermon on the Mount is by far the most popular sermon in all of history. Its message of hope appeals to everyone who read it. One need not be Christian in order to take solace in these wonderful words.

**The Sermon begins:**

**The Beatitudes**

Jesus said:

"Blessed are the poor in spirit, for theirs is the kingdom of heaven.

Blessed are those who mourn, for they will be comforted.

Blessed are the meek, for they will inherit the earth.

Blessed are those who hunger and thirst for righteousness, for they will be filled.

Blessed are the merciful, for they will be shown mercy.

Blessed are the pure in heart, for they will see God.

Blessed are the peacemakers, for they will be called children of God.

Blessed are those who are persecuted because of righteousness, for theirs is the kingdom of heaven.

 Blessed are you when people insult you, persecute you and falsely say all kinds of evil against you because of me.

Rejoice and be glad, because great is your reward in heaven, for in the same way they persecuted the prophets who were before you."

The Beatitudes are the core of the Sermon on the Mount, but not the only important part. Jesus goes on to solidify his teachings to embrace all aspects of life. The core of all his teachings is mindfulness, controlling the mind. Thinking deeply before doing something, even if it means you need to deviate from the law.

**Jesus Heals Many:**

At around sunset, the people brought Jesus pretty much all those who had various kinds of illnesses. It was here that he laid his hands on them and he healed them one by one. He performed many exorcisms and during these sessions the demons came flying out of people, declaring Jesus was the Son of God. In one instance the demons say "Go away! What do you want with us, Jesus of Nazareth? Have you come to destroy us? I know who you are—the Holy One of God!" Despite their declarations, Jesus rebuked them and would not allow them to speak. Everyone was amazed and said to each other, "What words these are! With authority and power he gives orders to impure spirits and they come out!"

After a full day of nonstop healing, Jesus wanted to withdraw from the people, to find a moment of peace. But it wasn't going to happen. The people were so desperate for salvation of all kinds that they would make his departure from them a bit difficult. Understandably weary, he kept on; he knew he had a mission to fulfill. Jesus says "I must proclaim the good news of the kingdom

of God to the other towns also, because that is why I was sent."
And he kept on preaching in the synagogues of Judea.

**Jesus Heals a Man With Leprosy:**

A man with leprosy comes up to Jesus and asks him for
healing.Begging, on his knees for Jesus to heal him. Jesus was
annoyed by this but healed him anyway. He warned the now
healed man "See that you don't tell this to anyone. But go, show
yourself to the priest and offer the sacrifices that Moses
commanded for your cleansing, as a testimony to them."

But no, that was not going to be, instead the man started spreading
the news of his healing. As a result, Jesus was so swamped with
requests for healings that he could no longer enter any town
openly, he had to stay in secluded areas outside the cities.But yet,
and the people still came to him from everywhere. Jesus could not
catch a break. Despite being the Lamb of God, he was still human
and he was exhausted. But it is not over.

**Jesus Forgives and Heals a Paralyzed Man**

A few days later, when Jesus went to Capernaum again, the people
heard that he had come. They gathered by the thousands, in fact the
large number of people created a situation where there was no
room left, not even out the door, and he preached the word to them.

Some people brought him a paralyzed man. Since they could not get close enough to Jesus because of the massive crowds, they made an opening in the roof right above Jesus. They made it large enough to lower the mat the man was lying on. When Jesus saw the intensity of their faith, he said to the paralyzed man, "Son, your sins are forgiven."

As in any large crowd, some of the people there did not like what they saw. Local rabbis, also know in the New Testament as "teachers of the law" were present, thinking to themselves, "Why does this fellow talk like that? He's blaspheming! Who can forgive sins but God alone?" In Jewish Scripture no one but God can forgive sin so the fact Jesus was forgiving people of their sins was outright blasphemy. This episode sowed the seeds for what was to come for Jesus.

Jesus was very aware of their presence and their inner thoughts. He said to them, "Why are you thinking these things? Which is easier: to say to this paralyzed man, 'Your sins are forgiven,' or to say, 'Get up, take your mat and walk'? I want you to know that the Son of Man has authority on earth to forgive sins." Jesus then turns to the paralyzed man and says, "I tell you, get up, take your mat and go home." Not surprisingly, the man got up, took his mat and walked out in front of the whole crowd. This amazed everyone and upon seeing this great miracles they declared, "We have never seen anything like this!"

**Jesus Eats with Sinners**

After all this, Jesus worked his way out and saw a tax collector by the name of Levi also known as Matthew sitting at his tax booth. "Follow me," Jesus said to him, and Matthew got up, left everything and followed him.

Matthew was so impressed with Jesus that he held a great banquet for Jesus at his house, in attendance was a large crowd of his tax collector friends as well as others. At this banquet, the chief rabbis of the sect called the Pharisees and the teachers of the law complained to Jesus' saying, "Why do you eat and drink with tax collectors and sinners?"

Jesus wisely answered them, "It is not the healthy who need a doctor, but the sick. I have not come to call the righteous, but sinners to repentance." Jesus' logic is incredibly sound.

**Jesus Is Lord of the Sabbath**

If fasting is a big deal in Judaism, observance of the Sabbath is an even bigger deal. There is more written about the Sabbath than most any other Jewish tradition. It is the day of rest, the day God took off after creation. It is a day dedicated to God.

One Sabbath, Jesus and his disciples were strolling through a grain field; they were hungry and began to pick some heads of grain. In Jewish Law this would be considered work and is strictly forbidden on the Sabbath. The Pharisees said to him, "Look, why are they doing what is unlawful on the Sabbath?"

He answered, "Have you never read what David did when he and his companions were hungry and in need? In the days of Abiathar the high priest, he entered the house of God and ate the consecrated bread, which is lawful only for priests to eat. And he also gave some to his companions." That is a great answer and so true. There wasn't much they could say.

Jesus doesn't stop there though; he goes on to say "The Son of Man is Lord of the Sabbath."

On another Sabbath he went into a synagogue and was teaching, while there, a man was there whose right hand was shriveled. The Pharisees and the teachers of the law knew Jesus could not refuse a chance to heal were looking for a reason to accuse Jesus, so they watched him closely to see if he would heal that man on the

Sabbath*. Jesus was very aware and knew what they were thinking and said to the man, "Get up and stand in front of everyone."

Then Jesus, looking right at the teachers of the law said "I ask you, which is lawful on the Sabbath: to do good or to do evil, to save life or to destroy it?"

Then said to the man, "Stretch out your hand." The mans hand was completely restored. Despite this great miracle, the Pharisees and the teachers of the law were furious and began plotting ways to get rid of Jesus.

*In Judaism it is perfectly legal to **save** a life on the Sabbath. If it is something that can wait until a weekday it must wait.

**Mary Magdalene**

Jesus went from one city and village to another preaching that the kingdom of God is at hand. During this time he had healed and ministered unto woman as well. Something that was scoffed at the chief priests and elders. He came in contact with one in particular, Mary Magdalene; she was said to be possessed by seven demons. Jesus cast them out of her. Not much is known about Mary Magdalene, but is clear that she becomes part of his entourage for she is present during the major agonies in Jesus' life.

## Jesus Instructs His Disciples

Around this time, Jesus officially gives his disciples authority to minster to the people and perform miracles. Before he bestows them with this great authority he warns them that they should only minister to the lost Sheep of Israel. Mainly other Jewish people. He told them to proclaim that the Kingdom of Heaven is at hand. He gave them full commission to heal the sick, raise the dead and cast out unclean spirits from the possessed. However, in so doing he mentions that they should bring no possessions save the cloths on their backs.

## Five Thousand Fed

At the end of that day, the disciples were tired, hungry and wanted to end the day in peace. They told Jesus to please send the crowds away. Jesus, however, had other plans. He ordered them to feed the entire crowd. The disciples were shocked at this order for they only had about 5 loaves of bread a couple of fish. It would take a miracle to feed five thousand people with that. Jesus with his intense faith raised the food up to heaven and produced enough food to feed the entire gathering of five thousand. This was truly one of the most memorable miracles he performs in the Gospels.

## Jesus Walks On Water

Right after he feeds the five thousand, Jesus sent the crowds away. Jesus told the disciples to fetch the boat while he went on a bit to be alone and to pray. While the disciples were on the boat the water becomes very rough. So rough they thought they would drown. Jesus being at the shore simply walked the turbulent water to the boat. At first the disciples thought it was a ghost. But no, it was Jesus himself. As he entered the boat, the winds stopped and the waters were calm

**Jesus reveals his true nature.**

A little over a week after the feed of the five thousand, Jesus took Peter, John and James to the mountain to pray. The three disciples dosed off. When they awoke they noticed Jesus had changed, his face radiated light, his cloths turned white and he was gleaming. The 3 disciples noted that he was talking to two people. Turns out he was talking to Moses and Elijah, the pillars of Judaism. Moses being the receiver of the Law and Elijah who was taken up bodily into heaven on a blazing chariot of fire. Suddenly a voice came from the heavens saying "This is My Son, My Chosen; Listen to him". When the voice went silent, Jesus was alone on the mountain once again, Moses and Elijah have departed. The three disciples did not tell a soul about this encounter.

The Rabbis of the time were starting to pay close attention to Jesus; he was starting to attract too much attention. This was bad news for them. Firstly because he was distracting people from what they thought Judaism was all about and secondly with this many people flocking to him he was gaining a lot of influence and all they needed was for Rome to start asking questions. Jesus knew this and several times over this period he foretells of his own death. He knew that day was going to come soon.

The time was coming for Jesus to make his final stand at Jerusalem. As the Prophecies foretell. The Messiah will be declared at Jerusalem.

# CHAPTER 5: A TRIUMPHAL ENTRY

The Moment has come; Jesus was now entering Jerusalem to be declared the Messiah. As they approached the Mount of Olives he sent two disciples to go into a surrounding village to get a donkey and colt and bring them to him. The disciples were concerned that they would get in trouble if they simply took the 2 beasts from their owners. Jesus however made it clear that the owners will part with these animals when they knew what they were needed for.

The crowds got wind of this and declared him the messiah. They shouted ""Hosanna to the Son of David; BLESSED IS HE WHO COMES IN THE NAME OF THE LORD; Hosanna in the highest!"

That was it; there was no turning back now. Jesus made a very public appearance as the messiah. As he entered the temple he caused a commotion by kicking out the money changers and merchants from the temple. He made it known the temple was meant as a house of prayer not a "Den of Robbers" as he put it. This act alone would have been very disruptive, catching the attention of all the high officially in the area. The chief rabbis saw what Jesus was doing and they became very concerned. But no reckoning was meant to be just yet.

At day break Jesus departed to spend the night at the city of Bethany. In the morning he returned to the temple and was immediately besieged with questions by the chief priest and elders. They questioned his authority. Jesus was very smart in answering their question with a question. Jesus said to them, "I will also ask you one thing, which if you tell Me, I will also tell you by what authority I do these things. "The baptism of John was from what *source,* from heaven or from men?" And they began reasoning among themselves, saying, "If we say, 'From heaven,' He will say to us, 'Then why did you not believe him?' "But if we say, 'From men,' we fear the people; for they all regard John as a prophet." And answering Jesus, they said, "We do not know." He also said to them, "Neither will I tell you by what authority I do these things." This was certainly not the answer they wanted. They knew if they could get him to say he was the messiah directly they could have him arrested for blasphemy. In either case, this inspired enough anger to target Jesus as a threat. His final moments await him.

# CHAPTER 6: MY GOD, MY GOD, WHY HAST THOU FORSAKEN ME?

All this was occurring around Passover time. This was a critical time and the high priests and elders were panicking about Jesus. They did not know what to do with him. They conspired to kill him. But they knew he was too popular and to do so during the Passover would cause a riot. They needed some way to get him. Little did they know they would find the person they needed to help them do just that.

**Enter Judas Iscariot**

Judas Iscariot was one of Jesus' disciples and had direct access to him. Judas suffering from a lack of judgment and greed offered to betray Jesus to the Rabbis for a fee. The rabbis were thrilled; they finally had someone willing to betray this person called Christ. They paid Judas 30 silver pieces.

**The Last Supper**

Jesus knew the end was near and desired to have his last Passover meal with his twelve disciples. As they were seated he looked around at them and said "Truly I say to you that one of you will betray me". The Disciples looking at each other in shock, proclaimed that they would never betray him. Each one asking "Truly Not I, Lord?" When

Judas asked, however, Jesus responds "You have said so". Jesus knew it would be Judas. Although Jesus knew he had to die in order to fulfill the prophecies of messiahship, he still condemned the act of betrayal as one of the worst things a person could do.

While they ate, Jesus took some bread and after blessing it as was customary, he broke the bread and gave a piece to each disciple stating " Take and eat of this bread; this is my body". When he took the wine he let them each sip of it saying "Drink from it for this is my blood of the covenant which is poured out for many for the forgiveness of sins". He went on to tell them that from this night forth he will no longer drink wine here but only when he is reunited with them in the kingdom of heaven.

After dinner they sang a praise of thanks which is customary and then walked to the Mount of Olives. As they went to the Mount of Olives he made an ominous prediction. He said "You will all fall away because of me this night, for it is written" I will stroke down the shepherd, and the sheep of the flock will be scattered". Peter immediately responded stating he would never, ever betray him. Jesus looks at him and says, "Truly I say to you that this very night you, before the rooster crows, you will betray me three times." Peter of course denies this will happen; the other disciples also vehemently denied any such notion of betrayal. But Jesus knew the truth.

## The Garden of Gethsemane

When they arrived at the Garden of Gethsemane which is located in the Mount of Olives ,Jesus desired to be alone so he could pray. He went a bit away from them, only taking Peter and the 2 sons of Zebedee and confessed that he was deeply grieved to the point of death. He brought them in order to watch over him as he walked a few more yards to pray on his own.

As he prayed he fell to his knees in fervent prayer to God saying " My Father, if it is possible, please let this cup pass from me, but yet no as I will, but thine will be done". Jesus was clearly afraid of what was to come.  But he knew, deep inside he had to go through with this. It was, for lack of a better term...his fate. When he finished his prayers he returned to Peter and the two sons of Zebedee and saw that they were asleep. He in aggravation rebuked them "So, you men could not keep watch with Me for one hour? "Keep watching and praying that you may not enter into temptation; the spirit is willing, but the flesh is weak." Still anxious he went away a second and third time to pray and asked God to relieve him of this destiny and again when he returned he found them sleeping.

## Jesus' Betrayal and Arrest

Before he could finish talking, Judas appeared with a large well armed crowd which included the chief priests and the elders of the people. Judas gives Jesus a kiss to indicate to the crowd that he was the one they wanted. At this point they seized him and his path to crucifixion began. During the commotion however one of Jesus' disciples took out a sword and cut off the ear of a servant of the high priest. But Jesus did not want violence and told the man to put his sword away.

**Jesus Stands Before The High Priest Caiaphas**

He was led away to be grilled by the High Priest Caiaphas in the presence of the elders. Peter didn't walk with them but followed from a distance but still able to witness the questioning of Jesus.

It was apparent from the start of this inquisition that the priests and elders would play dirty. They tried to coax people into giving false testimony against Jesus, but the accounts did not match. Jesus all the while remained silent. The high priest in extreme annoyance yells out "I adjure you by the living God, that you tell us whether you are the messiah, the son of God". Jesus answers ""You have said it yourself; nevertheless I tell you, hereafter you will see THE SON OF MAN SITTING AT THE RIGHT HAND OF POWER, and COMING ON THE CLOUDS OF HEAVEN."

By Jewish standards his statement was incredibly blasphemous, so much so that the high priest tore his robe in anger. That alone was enough for him, no witnesses needed to be called. Jesus condemned himself in their eyes. The high priest turns to the crowd and asks "What do you think?" They all cry out "He deserves death". At this point they converged upon Jesus, spitting on him and slapping him, mocking him all the while.

## Peter Denies Jesus

As Peter stood there witnessing this horrible trial, people recognized him and identified him as being a follower of Jesus. Peter denied their claims saying he did now know who Jesus was. This happened...3 times, just as Jesus predicted. Then a rooster crowed and Peter Suddenly remembered what Jesus predicted and started to cry bitterly.

## Judas Regrets His Decision

As morning broke the chief priest and elders started the process to deliver Jesus to Pontius Pilate, a high ranking magistrate, governor of Judea. At this time, Judas appears before the priests and finds out that Jesus will be condemned to death. His heart sinks and he feels great remorse. He flung the 30 pieces of silver at their feet and departed. Later that day, he hanged himself. His betrayal of Jesus was just too much for him to handle.

## Jesus Stands Before Pilate.

Now Jesus had to endure another grilling, this time by Pontius Pilate. Pilate asks Jesus "Are you the King of the Jews?" Jesus responds with his often short answers "It is as you say". Pontius did not think much of this and was inclined to let him go, however during Passover it was customary for the governor to pardon people based on requests from the crowd. So he displayed Jesus and a notorious criminal by the name of Barabbas in front of the people and asked" Who shall I spare, Jesus or Barabbas?"

But here is where the story takes an interesting twist. Pontius Pilate's wife whispered to him that she had a dream that he should not have any hand in the death of Jesus. Pontius was able to let him go, but the chief priest and elders persuaded the crowd to request the death of Jesus and the immediate release of Barabbas.

Pilate really did not want to execute Jesus, but at the same time he didn't want a riot to form. So he took some water and washed his hands in front of the crowd saying "I am innocent of this man's blood, see to that yourselves". The people in their haste and rage were completely okay with that. They cried out "His blood shall be on us and our children". Little did they know this statement would be taken very literally later in history. Pilate released Barabbas as they requested. Jesus was then whipped mercilessly and was sent on his way to crucifixion.

**Jesus Is Mocked As He is Prepared For Death**

As commanded, the soldiers prepared Jesus for execution. The Roman soldiers known for their barbaric torturous ways did not spare Jesus. They stripped him of his cloths, placed on him a scarlet robe and a crown made out of thorns and placed a reed in his hands as if he were a Cesar and humiliated him; kneeling before him in mock reverence saying " Hail King of the Jews". They spat on him and beat him on his head. After this horrible episode they took the scarlet robe off and put its own cloths back on and led him to his crucifixion.

*The Crucifixion*

With a crucifix on his back, they arrive at a place called Golgotha or Place of the skulls and stop. He was mocked further, they gave him wine mixed with gall (something bitter) which was so foul Jesus did not care to drink any further.

They lay the cross on the ground, position Jesus and proceed to nail his wrists and feet to the cross. No doubt, crucifixion was by far one of the worst deaths to endure. They placed above his head the charges against him; it said "This is Jesus, The King of the Jews"

Even unto his death he was not spared humiliation, besides being crucified alongside two criminals, people at the base of the cross mocked him saying "If you are king of the Jews, son of God, save yourself." And even worse, the criminals who were crucified alongside him mocked him, forgetting their own misery for a moment.

Night was falling; Jesus was already on the cross for several hours. In a moment of torment Jesus cries out " "ELI, ELI, LAMA SABACHTHANI?" that is, "MY GOD, MY GOD, WHY HAVE YOU FORSAKEN ME?"

Jesus lets out one more cry and at that moment ...Jesus dies. He was 33 years old.

At that moment, through miraculous means, the veil of the temple was torn in two from the top to the bottom and an earthquake shook the land. This earthquake was said to have opened the tombs of the saints. Then, it is said, that the dead saints rose from the ground. After seeing this, a Roman officer knew, they did, in fact, kill the son of God.

# CHAPTER 7: THE RESURRECTION

**Jesus is Buried**

In the evening, a rich disciple of Jesus by the name of Joseph from Armiathea went to Pontius Pilate and asked that he be given the body of Jesus. The request was granted. Joseph had Jesus' body wrapped and placed in his own tomb that was carved out of the face of a large rock. He rolled a boulder in front of the tomb and left. Mary Magdalene and as the bible put it "'The other Mary" were seated by the tomb mourning.

Jesus, during his ministry stated that three days after his death he will raise again. The chief priests and elders did not believe this claim, but they were afraid that his disciples might play a trick and remove his body from the tomb and proclaim that the body is not there because Jesus resurrected. They quickly went to Pilate and asked if they had permission to have guards watch the tomb so this would not happen. They received permission and with utmost care they made sure that no one could come in or out of the tomb.

**Jesus Has Risen**

After the Sabbath, both Marys' came to visit the tomb of Jesus. At that moment a strong earthquake struck and an angel of God appeared to them and rolled away the stone from the tomb and sat on it. The guards saw this in fear and fainted, the bible states "...they became like dead men". Both Marys' also seized with fright did not know what to do. The angel assured them saying "Do Not be afraid; for I know that you are looking for Jesus who has been crucified. He is not here, for He has risen, just as he said..." The angel went on to say that Jesus went to Galilee and that they should rush on their way there so they may see him. They fled the tomb with great fear and ran to report this miracle to the 11 disciples. On the way, Jesus appears to the Marys' and comforts them, and tells them to fetch the other disciples so they too can see him.

The guards eventually wake up, run to the city to report to the chief priest and elders what they experienced. The chief priests were alarmed and knew if this news went public this would cause a riot. They eventually bribe the guards to keep quiet about the truth and to spread lies stating the disciples came at night and stole the body of Jesus.

**His Final Appearance**

His disciples arrive at Galilee and there he was, Jesus in full form. This was such a shocking event that some of the disciples doubted this event. Could it really be? Yes, it was true, it was Jesus himself. At this last gathering he says his final words to them "All authority has been given to me in heaven and on earth. Go therefore and make disciples of all the nations, baptizing them in the name of the Father and the Son and the Holy Spirit, teaching them to observe all that I commanded you; and lo, I am with you always, even to the end of the age."

# CONCLUSION

There is little doubt that Jesus was the most important figure in western history, his life and teachings paved the way and laid the foundation for the western world. Some would say that is a bad thing. Some say Jesus didn't exist at all. No one can deny that this person, who we call Jesus, changed the world forever...No matter what side they take.

# ABOUT THE AUTHOR

Doron Alon is the Best Selling author of 50 books and founder of Numinosity Press Inc.

He writes on a wide variety of topics including History, Self-help, Self-Publishing, and Spirituality. His conversational writing style and his ability to take complex topics and make them easily accessible has gained him popularity in the genres that he writes for.

To learn more about his other books on a wide variety of topics please visit http://www.doronalon.com or visit his author page at Amazon to find out more.

http://www.amazon.com/author/doronalon

Interviewswithhistory.com

# ABOUT THE SERIES

The goal of the Interviews With History series is to provide concise biographical information for people who want to read biographies, but do not have the time to read hundreds of pages or purchase expensive study courses. What you read in an Interviews With History Title are the pertinent facts; no filler. Written in an easy to understand and conversational fashion. To learn about future releases in this series please visit www.interviewswithhistory.com